Dr K M A Ahamed Zubair

Arabic and Persian Learning in Tamil Nadu

Dr K M A Ahamed Zubair

Arabic and Persian Learning in Tamil Nadu

Arabic and Persian Scholarship in South India during the British and Post-Independence Periods

Noor Publishing

Imprint

Any brand names and product names mentioned in this book are subject to trademark, brand or patent protection and are trademarks or registered trademarks of their respective holders. The use of brand names, product names, common names, trade names, product descriptions etc. even without a particular marking in this work is in no way to be construed to mean that such names may be regarded as unrestricted in respect of trademark and brand protection legislation and could thus be used by anyone.

Cover image: www.ingimage.com

Publisher:
Noor Publishing
is a trademark of
Dodo Books Indian Ocean Ltd. and OmniScriptum S.R.L publishing group

120 High Road, East Finchley, London, N2 9ED, United Kingdom
Str. Armeneasca 28/1, office 1, Chisinau MD-2012, Republic of Moldova, Europe
Printed at: see last page
ISBN: 978-620-7-47851-4

Arabic and Persian Learning in Tamil Nadu

Arabic and Persian Scholarship in South India during the British and Post-Independence Periods

Dr.K.M.A.Ahamed Zubair

Associate Professor of Arabic, The New College,

Chennai 600 014, India

اللغة العربية تحمل كلمة الله، وروح محمد ﷺ، وسر الإسلام،

This work has been dedicated to the Indian Islamic Missionaries

(1500-1800)

Preface

In the rich tapestry of India's cultural history, Arabic and Persian have woven themselves as vibrant threads, influencing the intellectual landscape for centuries. The following passages delve into the profound legacy of Arabic and Persian scholarship in South India, tracing their journey through the annals of time. From the bustling centers of Arcot, Vellore, Madras, to the scholarly hub of Natharnagar, these languages have flourished, nurturing generations of learners with their profound wisdom and poetic elegance. As we embark on this exploration, may we gain a deeper appreciation for the enduring significance of Arabic and Persian in shaping the intellectual and cultural fabric of our nation.

Dr K M A Ahamed Zubair

Contents

Introduction:

Amidst the bustling cities and serene towns of South India, a rich tradition of Arabic and Persian scholarship has thrived, illuminating the minds of scholars and enthusiasts alike. Through the passages ahead, we embark on a journey to uncover the remarkable journey of these languages, from their origins to their contemporary relevance. The narrative unfolds with a meticulous exploration of historical figures and educational institutions that have served as bastions of Arabic and Persian learning. We delve into the lives of eminent scholars, tracing their contributions to literature, academia, and cultural exchange. Moreover, we examine the evolving landscape of Arabic and Persian education in South India, noting the increasing interest and engagement among both Muslim and non-Muslim communities. As we navigate through the corridors of time, may we gain a deeper understanding of the profound impact of Arabic and Persian on the intellectual heritage of South India.

Arabic and Persian Learning in Tamil Nadu

Arabic and Persian Scholarship in South India during the British and Post-Independence Periods

UNDER BRITISH RULE AND POST INDEPENDENCE PERIOD (1857-1960 A.H.)

During British rule and the post-independence period (1857-1960), significant events occurred. Following the death of Nawab Ghulam Ghouse Khan in 1272 A.H. (1855 A.D.), the British Government dismissed servants with less than twelve years of service, providing pensions to senior officials and long-serving servants. Nawab Azeemjah was appointed Prince of Arcot with a monthly allowance starting from January 1, 1867 A.D. The Nawab's court was closed and sealed on April 7, 1857 A.D., and the Court of the Promulgation of Orders was shut down on January 1, 1858 A.D. Commissioners were tasked with assessing debts owed by the deceased Nawab, and native soldiers were disbanded and replaced by company soldiers. Government Agent Edward Balfour sealed the Nawab's offices on November 22, 1856 A.D., and records were removed on January 18, 1857 A.D. The Nawab's personal properties were auctioned to settle debts, and a Receiver was appointed by the Madras Government on

June 14, 1859 A.D., to oversee the Nawab's estates. Subsequently, items like the golden throne and staircase meant for Mecca were auctioned off, along with properties like Khas Bagh and Shadi Mahal. The Income Tax Act, introduced on December 1, 1860 A.D., faced strong opposition from the populace.

Scholars, writers, and poets, who had been receiving patronage from the Nawabs, opted to leave the region and seek employment elsewhere. Many migrated to Hyderabad, settling there. Here are the names of some notable scholars who departed for Hyderabad on the specified dates:

1. Moulvi Muhammad Mahdi Wasif (22nd Zulhaj 1270 A.H.)
2. Syed Abdul Wahab Husaini (18th Rabiul Awwal 1271 A.H.)
3. Moulvi Habeebullah Zaka (1271 A.H.)
4. Husain Ahmad Khan (2nd Shaban 1271 A.H.)
5. Muhyuddin Husain Khan and others (11th Jamadiul Akhar 1273 A.H.)
6. Hakeem Qudrat Nabi, son-in-law of Qazi Irtaza Ali Khan (12th Jamadiul Akhar 1274 A.H.)
7. Najaf Ali Khan and
8. Moulvi Yahya Ali Khan Nudrat, brother of Qazi Irtaza Ali Khan (17th Shawwal 1274 A.H.)

9. Moulvi Abdul Ali, son of Moulvi Muhammad Mahdi Wasif (4th Rabiul Awwal 1276 A.H.)

10.   Mustaqeem Jung (19th Zulhaj 1274 A.H.)

11.   Mir Raza Ali Khan (9th Rabius Sani 1276 A.H.)

12.   Hakeem Maseehuddowlah (16th Shawwal 1277 A.H.)

13.   Moulvi Mufti Yousuf Ali Khan (17th Jamadiul Akhar 1277 A.H.)

14.   Khawja Mohyuddin Saheb (24th Muharram 1280 A.H.)

15.   Shah Ali Saheb (1st Shaban 1280 A.H.)

16.   Moulvi Muhammad Husain Raqim (24th Muharram 1285 A.H.)

17.   Mir Mahdi Thaqib (3rd Janadiul Awwal 1285 A.H.)

18.   Moulvi Mufti Muhammad Sayeed and

19.   Moulvi Husain Ataullah, sons of Qazi Badruddowlah (5th Rahbius Sant 1286 A.H.)

20.   Moulvi Shahabaddin (24th Jamadins Sani 1290 A.H.)

Some of them returned to Madras, while others permanently settled there. The names and dates mentioned above were extracted from the personal diaries maintained by Moulvi Abdul Wahab Madarul Umara Bahadur, Qazi Badruddowlah Bahadur, and their sons. Many of them passed away in Hyderabad but maintained connections with the people and scholars of Madras. Most of their books were printed and published in Madras.

Madrasa-e-Azam, established in 1268 A.H. (1851 A.D.) by Nawab Ghulam Ghouse Khan Bahadur as an Arabic and Persian institution, was converted into an English High School on May 1, 1859 A.D. Teachers such as Moulvi Shahabuddin, Moulvi Muhammad Hayat, Haji Imamuddin, Syed Muhammad Husain Tamanna, Moulvi Syed Murtaza, Syed Muhammad, Moulvi Syed Mahmood, and Hakeem Muhammad Ali Sayeed, known as Hakeem Haziq Yar Khan Bahadur, were employed to teach Arabic, Persian, Islamic Theology, and Unani medicine. However, they were gradually removed and dismissed. Qazi Badruddowlah and his associates vehemently opposed the inclusion of secular subjects in the curriculum but their protests were ignored. The new authorities aimed to overhaul the educational system, promoting English and local languages over Arabic and Persian. Schools emphasizing secular education were established, sidelining the teaching of Muslim theology and religion. Moulvi Muhammad Hayat, a dedicated Arabic teacher, moved to Hyderabad and became a teacher at Dar-ul-Uloom, where he passed away on January 17, 1873 A.D. Moulvi Mufti Yousuf Ali Khan also died in Hyderabad on October 6, 1864 A.D. Moulvi Shahabuddin, appointed as a teacher at Madrasa-e-Kalan, Madras, was another individual affected by these changes.

After the passing of his teacher, Malikul Ulama Moulvi Alauddin Ahmad in 1242 A.H., spent nearly 58 years dedicated to teaching. He passed away on Monday, the 10th of Ramadhan, 1300 A.H. (July 16, 1883 A.D.), and was laid to rest within the grounds of the Walajahi

Mosque in Madras. The East India Company operated its own Madrasa within Fort Saint George, Madras, where Moulvi Turab Ali Nami and Moulvi Muhammad Hasan All Mahali taught Arabic and Persian. Numerous works in Arabic and Persian were published by this institution. However, this policy changed over time, and the Madrasa was eventually transformed into a high school. After several years, it evolved into a college, now known as Presidency College, Madras. Muslims were aware of these transformative strategies employed by the English. Muslim scholars and writers, acting as private tutors, were already engaged in teaching Arabic and Persian to students. They began establishing Madrasas one after another across South India.

Al-Madrasa al-Aroosia

In the far south, an Arabic Madrasa was established and overseen by Imam-al-Aroos, Syed Mohammad Mapillay Labbai Alim Saheb (1232-1316) of Kilakkarai. He was the son-in-law of Takya Abdul Qadir Saheb (1192-1267) of Kilakkarai. Familiarly called "Mapillay Alim Saheb," he earned the nickname "Imam-al-Aroos," meaning "bridegroom Allm Saheb," due to his marriage. His Madrasa became known as al-**Madrasat-al-Aroosia**. It flourished under his guidance, attracting around four hundred students from South India and Ceylon. However, with the rise of English education, its significance dwindled. It now functions as a standard Madrasa, offering instruction in Arabic and Islamic theology to interested learners.

Syed Muhammad was undoubtedly a notable educator and literary figure of his time. His mother, Amina, hailed from the lineage of Shaikh Sadaqatullah Appa, being the daughter of Miran Umma, who was the daughter of Shaikh Sadaqatullah, the son of Shaikh Sulaiman, the son of Qazi-al-Quzat.

Shaikh Mohammad Labbai Alim, son of Shaikh Sadaqatullah Appa, had a lineage tracing back to Vellai Ahmad, son of Miran Labbal, grandson of Ahmad, great-grandson of Sadaqa, and so forth. "Vellai" meaning "white" in Tamil symbolized purity.
His son remarked: "Among people, he was called 'white' for he whitens hearts from darkness and ugliness."

Ahmad, Vellai Ahmad's grandfather, was so immersed in mystical fervor that he constantly wandered in a state of ecstasy, wearing out his sandals, earning him the epithet "Breaker of the sandals of being the other.'"

Syed Mohammad was born on the 18th of Muharram, 1232 A.H., in Kayalpatnam, the same residence where Shaikh Sadaqatullah Appa lived before moving to Kilakkarai. His family relocated when he was two. At ten, he memorized the Holy Quran and initiated Arabic studies under his father, recalling:

"My childhood days resembled my siblings' until we completed memorizing the Quran by the age of ten. We learned grammar, syntax, and jurisprudence, guided solely by our father."

In his youth, he struggled with a stammer. His father sent him to Shaikh Mohammad al-Nuski, who recited Quranic verses, breathed into his mouth, offered honey, and water, easing his speech impediment. Syed Mohammad later studied under Takya Abdul Qadır Saheb of Kilakkarai, avidly attending lectures and communal prayers. He excelled in Arabic language and literature, earning the respect of his teacher.

He possessed a strong conviction that he would one day attain a distinguished and esteemed position. Consequently, he made the decision, despite opposition from his wife, to marry off his fourth daughter, Sara Ummal. The wedding took place on the 27th of Rabl-al-Akhar in the year 1253 A.H. Syed Mohammad remained devoted to his revered teacher until the teacher's passing in 1267 A.H. He then assumed leadership of the Qadriya order in South India and Ceylon, touring extensively to enroll numerous followers into his order.

During a business trip to Ceylon in 1252 (1835 A.D.), he observed the backwardness of Muslims, particularly in religious studies, and resolved to address this issue. He encouraged the establishment of mosques, madrasas, and takyas (reclusaries) and personally founded many such centers during subsequent visits to Ceylon. Notable establishments included the Maghnam-al-Suada in 1881, Bukhari Takya in 1883, Arcosiya Takya in 1885, and Maal-ul-Khairat in 1886, among others.

In addition to his role as a teacher and religious guide throughout his life, he actively fostered religious spirit among Muslims by organizing periodic gatherings for Zikr (remembrance of Allah) and prayers. His efforts aimed to enlighten and uplift the Muslim community spiritually and intellectually.

He authored several books in Tamil on Islamic theology and jurisprudence, having them printed in Arab Tamil script to assist those who were not fluent in Arabic. He made adjustments to the Arabic script to accommodate Tamil phonetics.

In 1287 A.H., at the age of fifty-five, he journeyed to Hejaz where he discovered a copy of his book, Minhat-al-Sarandib, in one of its libraries, bringing him immense joy. His travels extended to Syria, Iraq, Yemen, and Iran, where he garnered attention for his scholarly contributions to theology, mysticism, and his mastery of the Arabic language.

Syed Muhammad passed away on the 5th of Rajab, 1316 A.H. (November 20, 1898 A.D.), and was laid to rest in the Takya at Kilakkarai beside his father-in-law's grave.

Among his works, he left behind:

"Maghani Mulah-it-Tibyan fi Sharh-i-Maani Fath-id-Dayyan": This work, comprising an enlarged edition of his earlier writings on Islamic theology and jurisprudence, including "Fath-ul-Mateen," "Fath-us-Salam," and "Fath-ud-Dayyan," was published first from his Barakatiya Press in Kilakkarai in 1304 A.H. It was subsequently reprinted in Bombay in 1318, 1325, and 1345 A.H., and again in Madras from the Shakir Press in 1377 A.H. The introduction is in Arabic, while the remainder of the book is in Arab Tamil script.

Mr. Saifuddin J. Aniff Dorai, a Malay gentleman and former Headmaster of Zahiriya College, Colombo, translated Syed Mohammad's book "Fath-ud-Dayyan" into English, which was published in 1963 by the Fathud Dayyan Publication Committee, located at 6 Melbourne Avenue, Colombo-4.

Additionally, Syed Mohammad composed several other works, including:

"Hadya Malaise Maghani" (pp. 391-394): A Tamil poem comprising 66 verses, penned as a gift for his wife who requested a "Pon Malai" (Gold necklace). It contains valuable advice for women.

"Talal Fatiha" (Head Fatiha) (see Maghani pp. 403-416): A mixture of Arabic and Tamil verses, written in Arab Tamil script, seeking Allah's favor through the spiritual intercession of Hazrath Fatima Zahra and other Prophets and Saints. It includes descriptions of paradise and hell, intended for the benefit of common people in South India, Ceylon, and the Far East, often recited fervently at the conclusion of devotional gatherings.

In addition to these works in Tamil, Syed Mohammad authored an Arabic book:
"Mawahib-al-Majeed fi Manaqib-1-Shahil-Hameed" (pp. 258): A biographical account of Shaikh Shahul Hameed Meeran Abdul Qadir (d. 978 A.H.) of Nagore, divided into an introduction and six chapters detailing various aspects of his life.

The third chapter details his journey upon arriving in the land of Arabia and his travels within its territories, leading up to Nahor.
The fourth chapter narrates events from his entry into Nahor until his demise.
The fifth chapter chronicles events posthumously, acknowledging his miraculous feats.

The sixth chapter emphasizes the necessity for similar individuals in the field of monotheism.

This book was penned by Syed Mohammad in 1263 A.H. at the behest of Nawab Ghulam Ghouse Khan Bahadur.

The version published by Moulvi Tamim Saheb, Madras in 1349 A.H., lacks the sixth chapter, possibly due to the author's inability to complete the book as originally planned.

Other works by Syed Mohammad include:

"Minhat-us-Sarandip if Mawlad-al-Habib" (pp. 106-132): Depicts the virtues and moral excellences of the Prophet, to be recited during the early twelve days of Rabi-ul-Awwal. It features fluent language interspersed with Arabic verses composed by the author.

"Ahsan-al-Mawaiz wa Azyan-al-Malafiz": A compilation of 280 verses on moral and ethical subjects, completed on the 16th of Zul Hajja, 1290 A.H.

"Mawahib-al-Zain fi Manaqib-al-Hasanain" (pp. 133-153): Depicts the virtues of Imam Hasan and Imam Hussain, to be recited in the early ten days of Muharram. The author refrains from mentioning the ill-treatment inflicted upon them by their opponents, as it could lead to disparagement of some companions of the Prophet and their sons.

"Mawlid Zanjabeel-1-Sulafatin Quraishiyya Muthalibiyah fi Sajanjal-I-Mira'ti" (pp. 153-167): Provides a detailed account of the virtues of Hazrath Imam Shafai.

"Manaih-u-Rabbil Arbab fi Madaih-1-Qutub-l-Aqtab" (pp. 193-220): Praises the virtues of Shaikh Abdul Qadir Jeelani and shares personal experiences regarding the blessings received from the Shaikh during times of distress and suffering.

"Maraghib Ulil Alsun fi Manaqib-Il-Qutub-i-Abil Hasan" (pp. 225-240): Illustrates the virtues of Shaikh Abul Hasan Shazli (593-656 A.H.).

"Minhat-al-Bari fi Midhal-it-Bukhari" and "Nafhat-al-Bari-al-Samad fi Midhat-al-Bukhari al Syed" (pp. 293-351): Depicts the life and virtues of Syed Mohammad Bukhari (1144-1207 A.H.) of Cannanore.

"Mawlid Ata-ir-Rasool fit Midhat-i-Sakha-il-Batul" (pp. 43×19): Describes the life and virtues of Khawja Mueenuddin Chishti of Ajmer (d. 6th Rajab 633 A.H.).

"Mawahib-al-Rahman fi Manaqib-i-Hasan ibn Usman": Gives the life and virtues of Mohammad (1229/1814-1303/1886), son of Shaikh Makhdoomi, a notable scholar buried at Alutgama, Ceylon.

"Mawhibat - al - Mawahib fi Manqabat - al-Shaikh Takya Saheb" (pp. 215-240): Provides life sketches and virtues of Takya Abdul Qadir Saheb (1191 - 1272) of Kayalpatnam and his esteemed father Shaikh Umar (1163 - 1216).

He has eloquently praised the numerous excellent qualities of his parents. Here are a few verses quoted about his father:

"So, my father, Sheikh Ahmad, was always devoted, remembering the dead and his own impending death constantly. Neither trade, nor occupation, nor hunger, nor fatigue distracted him from the remembrance of his Lord. Neither family matters, nor worldly concerns, nor tiredness ever hindered him, nor did laziness oppose him for a day, nor did he indulge in idleness for a period. He stood up at night, weeping in fear for Him, reciting the Quran beautifully word by word. He often stayed awake with us, awakening us with what he whispered passionately, between silent prayers and audible longing, with sighs and moans, spending the night until he was called to success with a cry. Hope and fear resided within him, nestled in his heart like the wings of a bird resting on the ground, wholly dedicated to his Lord's deeds, always sincere in heart, devoid of flattery. When we praised him, he would fervently shout with love, as if intoxicated, drawn to the beloved. He was repeatedly overwhelmed and then composed, as if he were sitting next to the Messenger of Allah, experiencing ecstasy when he stood among us, admonishing and narrating, softer and more humbled, to the point where he would cry, making us cry too, shedding tears when he mentioned the horrors of Hell or the dreadful consequences of sin, cutting off worldly desires and severing ties with evil governance. His heart was entirely detached from this world, renouncing its pleasures, considering it worthless. He became averse to it, making its detriment his dowry in anticipation of its desecration, striving in the path of the Most Merciful with true dedication, effort, and acceptance of divine decree, confronting every enemy of our faith, fasting even in summer, performing ablution in the icy cold of a rainy snowstorm, fasting between the two evenings without speaking unnecessarily, engaging in constant prayers and other obligatory acts even during illness and health, pain and comfort. He was always engaged in abundant prayers upon the Prophet, like the constant liturgy of the dedicated servants of Allah."

About his mother:

"Her virtues have perfumed the universe; they spread so that multitudes could breathe their fragrance. There was nothing in the world more delightful to behold than her exemplary companionship, like the harmony of a pair of well-matched spouses. Often, I observed her praying behind him, remembering Allah with him for long stretches. Even though she prayed separately, she always repeated her prayers so that he would not pray alone, setting an example for him to pray behind her. She was punctual in observing times and steadfast in prioritizing them, fasting and standing in prayer, never missing a prayer or fast since she reached the age of maturity. She was consistent, without laziness, in reciting the Quran every morning and would complete two recitations every month, completing additional recitations during Ramadan. She would perform voluntary prayers as if they were obligatory, and would regularly recite eleven different portions of the Quran with her prayer beads. She was diligent in reciting the recommended invocations and supplications, having learned them from her husband's spiritual guide, whom she pledged allegiance to with complete devotion. From his teachings, she attained a distinguished status, and through her practice, she ignited the souls of her loved ones."

Once, an Arab visitor came to see him, impressed by his profound knowledge of theology, mysticism, and his mastery of the Arabic language. However, he sought to gauge his skill in poetic composition. Taking up his pen, he composed a lengthy poem of 76 lines, beginning with verses that praised the beauty of his countenance. He further lauded:

"How many have been captivated by his beauty,

Like a traveler lost in wonder,

When stung by a scorpion, it dies without a sound,

Yet its killer faces no retribution in our law.

So, how can they all be like slaves?"

She became adorned without jewels; indeed, the jewels were not worthy of her praise, as earrings and necklaces were displayed upon her like ice. She stood, her gaze fixed, igniting a fire in the hearts; when she departed, the flame she ignited did not extinguish. She left behind intoxicated lovers, ascending the stairs of her palace, where she appeared like an idol, while those around her, between admirers and devotees, prostrated.

The Arab was so enamored with this eloquent style that he exclaimed:

"By God! This is a clear Arabic language."

His distinguished sons, Abdul Qadir (1264-1331) and Shahul Hameed (1271-1339), known as Khalwat and Jalwat Nayagam respectively, zealously served Arabic education in the southernmost regions. Currently, the Madrasa is efficiently managed by Ahmad Abdul Qadir Sahib and Shuaib Alim Saheb, the son and grandson of Syed Shahul Hameed, respectively.

Moulvi Abdul Wahab (1247-1337)

He was a student of Syed Abdul Lateef of Vellore. Subsequently, he established a Madrasa in Vellore named Baqiyat-al-Salihat. He was the son of Moulvi Abdul Qadir, who was the son of Moulvi Ghulam Mohyuddin, who was the son of Moulvi Hafiz Abdul Qadir, who was the son of Moulvi Shah Madar. Shah Madar, his great-grandfather, was a spiritual guide who passed away in Madurai. His great-grandfather

Hafiz Abdul Qadir had memorized the entire Quran and dedicated his life to teaching Arabic and Persian to students. Hafiz Abdul Qadir also passed away in Madurai on 15th Jamadi-ul-Awwal 1173 A.H. Moulvi Ghulam Mohyuddin, Moulvi Abdul Wahab's grandfather, lived in Attur, a village in the Salem district, and passed away there on 8th Rabiul Awwal 1220 A.H. Abdul Qadir, Moulvi Abdul Wahab's father,

Abdul Wahab was born in Attur on the 15th of Rabiul Akhar 1198 A.H. He received his education in Arabic and Persian from his father and other teachers. Later, he obtained a certificate from Qazi Irtaza All Khan in Madras after studying under him for several years. He was initiated into the Qadriya order by Syed Shah Abul Hasan Mahvi Qadri of Vellore. At the suggestion of his spiritual guide, he married a second wife, Fatima Begum, and had a son named Abdul Wahab.

His Persian studies began under Moulvi Hakeem Zainul Abideen of Vellore, who practiced Unani medicine at that time. He continued his studies under Moulvi Ghulam Qadir, a student of Qazi Irtaza Ali Khan Bahadur, and Syed Shah Abdul Lateef of Vellore, who initiated him into the Qadriya order. He then traveled to the North to learn the art of debate from Moulvi Rahmatullah of Kerana, who later migrated to Mecca. Abdul Wahab also studied Traditions from Moulana Syed Husain, Muhaddis of Peshawar, during his time in Mecca.

Returning to India, Abdul Wahab was determined to dedicate his time and talents to spreading Islamic learning and theology. He established the Madrasa-Baqiyat-al-Salihat in Vellore in 1301 A.H. (1884 A.D.), and oversaw the construction of the building and mosque in 1304 A.H. (1887 A.D.), which were later renovated and expanded. In 1907 A.D. (1324 A.H.), he was honored with the title of Shamsul Ulama by the Indian Government.

Abdul Wahab focused on teaching Arabic and Persian to students throughout his life, prioritizing service to the people over personal wealth accumulation. Although he didn't compile many books, he wrote several brochures on theological topics. He was highly respected, and his death in Vellore on the 22nd of Rabius Sani.

On the 25th of January 1919 A.D., corresponding to the 23rd of Rabi II 1337 A.H., hundreds of people gathered in Vellore from all around to pay their last respects to Abdul Wahab. The mosque and Madrasa compound couldn't accommodate the crowd for the funeral prayer, so it was held in the open ground in front of the Vellore fort, with around ten thousand devotees participating. Abdul Wahab was then buried in the mosque and Madrasa campus.

Moulvi Abdus Samad Ilmi composed a short mathnawi titled "Samanistan," in which he identifies three mujaddids (renewers) of Islam in the last century: Haji Imdadullah Thanawi, Moulana

Mohammed Qasim Nanotvi, and Moulana Abdul Wahab Saheb. He praises Abdul Wahab for his contribution to spreading divine knowledge and reviving Islam, stating that his spiritual enlightenment radiated throughout the world, illuminating hearts and minds with the light of knowledge.

Khan Bahadur Moulvi Ziyauddin Mohd. succeeded his father Abdul Wahab as the head of the institution. He appointed Moulana Abdul Jabbar as the principal of Baqiyat-al-Salihat. Moulana Abdul Jabbar authored two works in Arabic: "Irshad-ul-Faj fi Anwar-il-Hajj" and "Al-Tanzech wal Tajreed fi Ithbat Wahdat-al-Wujud wal Tawheed" on Wahdat-ul-Wajud (Unity of Existence). He also composed a long poem in Arabic known as Qaseeda-e-Nuniya. Moulana Abdul Jabbar passed away on the 25th of Shaban 1353 A.H. (3rd December 1934 A.D.).

Following his demise, Moulana Abdur Raheen Saheb took over as the principal, and after him, Moulvi Haji Mufti Shaikh Adarn became the head. The institution continues to operate under the management of Sahukar A. Abdul Shukoor and Sahukar Abdul Jameel, with Moulvi Abu Bakr and his successors Syed Sibghatullah Bakhtiyari and Abdur Rahman al Fazfari serving as principals. The alumni of this Madrasa have spread across South India, Kerala, and Ceylon, actively promoting the study of Arabic language, Islamic theology, and jurisprudence, particularly through the Tamil medium. Several books on Quran, Prophet's traditions, jurisprudence, and Islamic biographies have been published by the alumni. Moulvi Abdul Kareem Baqvi initiated Misbah-al-Huda Madrasa in Nidur, Mayuram, in 1330 (1912), continuing the tradition of Arabic education. Another individual, Mohammed Abdul Kareem Baqvi, founded Al-Madrasat-al-Nur-al-Muhammadi in Pudukkudi near Kutanallur, Tanjore District, in 1334 (1916).

The founder of Al-Madrasat-al-Nur-al-Muhammadi passed away on the 4th of Zul Hijja in 1345 A.H. (25th May 1927) and was laid to rest within the compound of the Madrasa. This Madrasa, along with Riyaz-al-Jinan fi Uloom al-Adyan established in 1291 (1871) by Peer Mohd. Rawter in Pettai, Tirunelveli, and Manba-ul-ula established in 1310 (1892) by K. P. Abu Bakr Moulvi in Kutanallur, have been managed and continue to be managed by the Beqvis.

Darul Uloom Lateefia, Vellore (est. 1302 A.H.)

Another significant institution for the study of Arabic and Persian languages was initiated at Vellore by Syad Shah Ruknuddin Muhammad (1269-1325 A.H.), the son of Syed Shah Abdul Lateef Saheb (who passed away in Madina in 1289 A.H.), on the 5th of Jamadius Sani 1302 A.H. (23rd March 1885 A.D.). It was named "Darul Uloom Lateefiya" after his father Syed Shah Abdul Lateef of Vellore. Bahrul Uloom Moulana Muhammad Taqi of Lucknow was appointed as its first principal. Annual meetings were conducted, and reports were presented to the audience. The land where this Madrasa stands is still known as Hazrat Makan (the abode of revered teachers). The first convocation took place on the 19th of Shaban 1311 A.H. (26th February 1894 A.D.), attended by ten thousand people who were all generously provided meals. Several scholars delivered speeches during the event. Moulvi Syed Shah Fakhruddin Fakhri of Mylapore, Madras, emphasized the importance of integrating religious education with modern sciences in English. He recited verses in Persian and Urdu, highlighting the need to unite religion with worldly matters.

The sacrifice and altruism of one's existence, where do they come from?
When there's no source, how can there be a derivative?

For the destitute, whose world is not upright,
It's difficult to mend things with his hands.

Whoever told you to leave the world behind,
Such words, don't attach them to yourself.

Cutting the rope of connection to the world's means,
The dogs of the washerman have drowned, not the house or the water.

To rectify religion, the world is necessary,
Without the world, claiming religion is deceit and coercion.

If you study sciences without grasping the essence,
It's like learning to guide without compass.

And if you impress others with eloquence forcibly,
You become a tyrant in knowledge acquisition.

But until you have support from behind,
Beware, don't stray from the scholars' sight.

O prideful one, seek knowledge and wisdom,
Don't shun the burden of learning.

It's destiny that has advised you,
Never to miss gatherings of knowledge and ethics.

And parents should never let Satan teach their children English.

Several philanthropists, including Meddekar Muhammad Jafar, Pak Malagi Muhammad Usman, Meddekar Muhammad Ghouse, Chelappe Muhammad Ibrahim Saheb, Chilmkar Haji Shaikh Miran Saheb, and Bangi Qadir Basha Saheb, collaborated on a significant project to construct a magnificent building on the site where Syed Shah Hasan Qurbi and his son Syed Shah Abdul Lateef Zawqi once resided. The foundation of the current building was laid on Friday, the 19th of Zul

Qada, 1311 A.H., in the presence of a large gathering of scholars and common people, by Syed Shah Ruknuddin Muhammad.

Moulana Moulvi Abdul Jameel of Peshawar and Moulana Ahmad Hasan of Kanpur also served as teachers in this institution. Moulana Moulvi Hakeem Mohyuddin Husain Cheedah, who passed away on Friday, the 14th of Rajab, 1336 A.H. (26th April 1918 A.D.), studied at this institution and later became its Principal. He was a poet and wrote poems in both Persian and Urdu under the pen name of Anwar. He was a student and disciple of Mir Mahdi Thaqib in poetry. As Urdu language gained more popularity in the region, scholars and poets preferred it for expressing their thoughts and emotions. As a result, Arabic and Persian works became less prevalent.

Mohyuddin Husain Cheedah Anwar declined a lucrative job offer from Hyderabad and chose to serve at Madrasa-e-Lateefiya for a humble salary. He authored two works in Urdu: Safarnamah-e-Haramain (pp. 284), an account of his journey to Mecca and Medina performed in 1322 A.H. 1904 A.D. for the second time, and Tibb-e-Ruhani, parts I and II (pp. 104 and pp. 88). The first part was published in 1320, and the second part in 1326 A.H. Many distinguished scholars and poets in South India are alumni of Madrasa-e-Lateefiya, Vellore.

Under the personal guidance of Syed Shah Ruknuddin Muhammad Qadri, the said institution served the best interests of the countrymen.

Syed Shah Ruknuddin Muhammad Qadri was honored with the title of Shamsul Ulama by the Viceroy and Governor-General of India on 16th January 1887 A.D. He was succeeded by his son, Syed Shah Abdul Lateef (1298-1338 A.H.), who significantly contributed to the advancement of Muslim learning in South India. Syed Shah Abdul Lateef was conferred the title of Shamsul Ulama in 1916 A.D. Upon his death on the 19th of Zulhaj, 1338 A.H., his eldest son, Syed Shah Abdul Qadir (1324-1378), was entrusted with the spiritual guidance and rectorship of the Madrasa through a will. Presently, the institution is managed by Syed Shah Muhammad Baqir and Syed Muhammad Tahir B.A., the younger brothers of Syed Shah Abdul Qadir.

Madrasa-e-Sayeedia, Madras, was established in 1289 A.H. At Madras, Haji Muhammad Basha, along with his sons, played a significant role in the establishment and management of the institution.

It was recognized that teaching Muslim theology in Arabic and Persian at Madrasas would be ineffective without providing means of livelihood for the students. As the poet mentioned:

"Even if you provide knowledge to everyone, until there's provision for livelihood, what use is the adornment of this knowledge?"

During that time, Vaniyambadi was a hub for Muslim scholars and preachers. Philanthropic businessmen organized grand meetings, especially during the months of Rabiul Awwal and Rablus Sani, inviting eminent scholars to speak about the Prophet's life and the saints of Islam. They also engaged these scholars to educate the town's children.

One such scholar was Moulana Sher Ali, originally from Afghanistan, known as Moulana Sher Ali Wilayati. Upon visiting Vaniyambadi, he was urged by local businessmen to educate the town's children. Consequently, he became the principal of Madrasa Madan-al-Uloom, established in 1304 A.H.

It seems there was a vibrant educational scene in Vaniyambadi, with scholars like Moulana Sher Ali Wilayati playing a pivotal role. Moulana Abdullah, a student of Moulana Sher Ali, was detained in Vaniyambadi to serve at Madrasa-e-Madan-al-Uloom. After his passing, Moulana Abdul Majeed of Pungnur took over as principal. He had studied in various institutions across Northern India before returning to serve as a teacher and later principal at Madrasa-e-Madan-al-Uloom until his death in December 1937.

Madrasa-e-Mufeed-e-Am was transformed into an English school, but **Madrasa-e-Madan-al-Uloom** continues to function as an Arabic and Persian institution under the leadership of Afzalul Ulama Katib Muhammad Yousuf, who succeeded his late father Moulana Katib Ibrahim Sahib.

In Madras, Qazi Badruddowlah and his brother Moulvi Abdul Wahab Madarul Umara dedicated themselves to Arabic, Persian, and theological education, not only for their own children and relatives but also for students from the city. Their selfless service inspired many of their students to become teachers themselves, continuing the tradition of education and mentorship without seeking any financial gain.

Tirazish Khan Bahadur, a notable figure in education, was instrumental in founding Madrasa-e-Muhammadi in Madras. He was a respected teacher who imparted knowledge to many students, including prominent individuals like Moulvi Ahmad Ali, Moulvi Mufti Mahmood, Moulvi Haji Ahmad, Moulvi Qazi Ubaidullah, Moulvi Mohyuddin, Syed Muhammad Ali Saheb Mashayakh, Moulvi Zahid Husain Mehkari, Moulvi Abdul Qadir, Moulvi Abdul Majeed, and Moulvi Qudrat Haleem. These students received their diplomas under his guidance on significant dates, marking their academic achievements.

Tirazish Khan Bahadur was not only an educator but also a talented poet, known for his Persian verses written under the pen name of Ahsan. His poetry, corrected by Raqim and Waqif, was esteemed and quoted in various anthologies.

A group of distinguished individuals, including the sons of Qazi Badruddowlah and others such as Ghulam Mahmood Mustawfiyuddowlah, Haji Abdul Rahman Qismat Khan Bahadur, and Hafiz Muhammad, dedicated themselves to teaching, contributing significantly to the educational landscape of their time.

Moulvi Muhammad Abdullah Sadarat Khan Bahadur, a notable figure in education and scholarship, dedicated his life to teaching Arabic and Persian. Born on 28th Rabiul Awwal 1236 A.H., he served as Sadrus Sudur during Nawab Ghulam Ghouse Khan Bahadur's reign, fulfilling roles as Mufti and Qazi in his father Qazi Badruddowlah's absence during pilgrimage. However, after Nawab Ghulam Ghouse Khan Bahadur's death in 1272 A.H., he was dismissed from service but granted a pension.

He spent his remaining years engrossed in reading, writing, and teaching, particularly focusing on copying significant works in Arabic and Persian for his personal library. His scholarly pursuits took him on multiple pilgrimages to Mecca and Medina, with his final journey in 1287 A.H. Sadly, he fell ill on his return to India and passed away in Gulbarga on Wednesday the 25th Rabiul Awwal 1288 A.H. = 14th June 1871 A.D.

Among his contributions are:

Fawaid-al-Ghawsiya fi Fur-uish Shafiya: His notes on Mukhtasar Abi Shuja, completed on Monday the 15th Muharram 1279 A.H.

Falz-ul-Bari fi Takhreej Ahadith-al-Baizawi: A work tracing the original references of Traditions in Baizawi's Quran commentary, completed up to the chapter of Taha (سورة طه).

Tuhfat-al-Ahibba fi Bayan Istihbab Qatl-al-Wazagha: A Persian work discussing the recommendation of killing lizards, completed in Persian.

The dedication to education and scholarship extended to several individuals from notable families. Ghouse Intizam Khan Bahadur, Husain Lutfullah, Ghulam Ahmad Qasim Jung, and Ghulam Muhammad Sharafuddowlah Bahadur, sons of Moulvi Abdul Wahab Madarul Umara, along with Haji Safiuddin Muhammad, Haji Muhammad, Haji Muhammad Abdullah, and Moulvi Muhammad Habeebullah, sons of Haji Qadir Murtaza Husain Salarul Mulk, all contributed their time to teaching Arabic and Persian.

One prominent figure, Moulvi Muhammad Abdullah Sadarat Khan Bahadur, born on 28th Rabiul Awwal 1236 A.H., served as Sadrus Sudur during Nawab Ghulam Ghouse Khan Bahadur's reign. He acted as Mufti and Qazi during his father Qazi Badruddowlah's pilgrimage in 1266-1267 A.H. Following Nawab Ghulam Ghouse Khan Bahadur's death in 1272 A.H., he was relieved from service and granted a pension. He devoted his remaining years to reading, writing, and teaching, emphasizing the copying of significant works in Arabic and Persian for his personal library. Despite multiple pilgrimages to Mecca and Medina, his final journey in 1287 A.H. resulted in illness during his return to India. He passed away in Gulbarga on Wednesday the 25th Rabiul Awwal 1288 A.H. = 14th June 1871 A.D.

His scholarly legacy includes:

Fawaid-al-Ghawsiya fi Fur-uish Shafiya: Notes on Mukhtasar Abi Shuja, completed on Monday the 15th Muharram 1279 A.H.

Falz-ul-Bari fi Takhreej Ahadith-al-Baizawi: A work tracing the original references of Traditions in Baizawi's Quran commentary, completed up to the chapter of Taha (سورة طه).

Tuhfat-al-Ahibba fi Bayan Istihbab Qatl-al-Wazagha: A Persian work discussing the recommendation of killing lizards, completed in Persian. he passed away before completing it. Moulvi Mufti Muhammad Sayeed's contributions in Arabic, Persian, and Urdu spanned diverse fields, including theology, Hadith compilation, and mathematics.

His Urdu book on mathematics, "Naseer-al-Hussab" (نصير الحساب),
demonstrates his versatility and commitment to spreading knowledge
across various disciplines.

Moulvi Mufti Muhammad Sayeed's scholarly endeavors extended
beyond his native Madras, as he relocated to Hyderabad in 1286 A.H.
at the invitation of Nawab Mukhtarul Mulk Salar Jung Bahadur. There,
he served as Mufti-é Sadr-e-Adalat (مفتى صدر عدالت) until his demise on
10th Shaban 1312 A.H.

Among his notable works are:

Al-Tanbeeh bit Tanzeeh (التنبيه بالتنزيه) in Arabic, published in 1309
A.H., addresses controversial theological issues related to God and His
attributes, critiquing the views of Imam Ibn Tymiyyah and his
followers.

Tashyeed-al-Mabani fi Takhreej Ahadith Maktubat Imam Rabbani
(تشنيد المبانى فى تخريج احاديث مكتوبات امام ربانى) in Arabic, published in 1311
A.H., focuses on compiling Hadiths from the writings of Imam
Rabbani.

Hidayat-al-Thiqat ila Nisab-al-Zakat (هداية الثقات الى نصاب الزكاة) in
Arabic, which deals with the regulations of Zakat.

Takhreej Ahadith-al-Atraf (تخريج احاديث الاطراف) in Arabic, and Al-Qawl-al-Jali fi Mana Qadami ala Raqbat-i-Kull-i-Wall (في القول الجلى) also in Arabic. (معنى قدمى على رقبة كل ولى

Risalah-e-Shaqqil Qamar (رساله شق القمر) in Persian, written in Ramadhan 1279 A.H., and Minhaj-al-Adalat (منهاج العدالت) are among his other works.

Despite his significant contributions, he couldn't complete his father's commentary on the Quran in Urdu, titled "Kareem فيض الكريم," before his passing.

Sirat-ul-Nabi (فيض الوهاب في سيرة النبى) in Persian, a biography of the Prophet Muhammad, in 1310 A.H. Moulvi Haji Ahmad Madani's contributions in various languages reflect his dedication to scholarship and his commitment to preserving historical and religious knowledge.

He also authored "Tarikh-e-Ahmadi" (تاريخ احمدى) in Persian, chronicling the history of his ancestors. Additionally, he compiled his father's judicial decrees into "Fatawa-e-Sibghiyya" (فتاوى صبغيه). Furthermore, he completed "Faiz-al-Wahhab fi Sirat-ul-Nabi" (فيض الوهاب في سيرة النبى), a biography of the Prophet Muhammad, in Persian in 1310 A.H.

Moulvi Haji Ahmad Madani's endeavors in Arabic, Persian, and Urdu literature underscore his multifaceted scholarship and his invaluable contributions to Islamic scholarship and historical documentation.

Moulvi Haji Mufti Mahmood's contributions in mathematics, astronomy, and Islamic education were significant. He was proficient in various fields and made notable advancements in his lifetime. He meticulously prepared charts detailing the timings of sunrise, sunset, prayers, and fasting, demonstrating his expertise in practical astronomy. His expertise was sought for determining the correct direction of the Qibla during mosque construction projects.

Moreover, Mufti Mahmood, along with Moulvi Abdullah Ahqar, crafted exquisite sun dials and astrolabes, showcasing their craftsmanship and dedication to precision. These artifacts, some of which still exist, serve as a testament to their skill and ingenuity. Notably, a bronze sun dial crafted by them adorns the mosque in Pulicat.

Mufti Mahmood's passing on December 16th, 1926, marked the end of an era, but his legacy lives on through his numerous works in Arabic, Persian, and Urdu. His contributions enriched Islamic scholarship and scientific knowledge, leaving an indelible mark on the intellectual landscape of his time.

Mufti Mahmood's contributions in Arabic literature are diverse and significant. Here are some of his notable works:

"Sharh Hashiya Abdullah Yazdi" - A commentary on logic, demonstrating his proficiency in philosophical discourse.

"Al-Silk-ul-Muazzam-al-Addurril Munazzam" - A commentary on "Ad-Durr-al-Munazzam" by Hafiz Muhammad Mazhar Naqshbandi, showcasing his expertise in Islamic scholarship and commentary.

"Mirat-al-Awqat wal Qibla" - A work on timekeeping and determining the Qibla direction, reflecting his knowledge in Islamic sciences.

"Tashreeh-al-Maani li Hirzil Amani" - A commentary on "Hirz-al-Amani," a poem by Imam Shatibi on Quranic recitation, illustrating his understanding of Quranic studies.

"Al-Hizb-al-Afkham fi Manqabat-al-Ghaws-al-Azam" - A short biography of Abdul Qadir Jeelani, demonstrating his devotion to Sufism and Islamic spirituality.

"Risalatun fi al-Manahi" - An article addressing the innovation of Muharram, showcasing his engagement with contemporary Islamic issues.

"Al-Tashreeh lit Talweeh" - Although incomplete, this work intended to be a commentary on the principles of Islamic jurisprudence, highlighting his interest in legal studies.

"Asma-ur-Rijal" - A biographical sketch of narrators of Traditions, reflecting his involvement in Hadith studies.

"Al-Jawharatus Saniyya ft Tahqeeq al-Niyyat" - A work on clarifying intentions, demonstrating his focus on spiritual and ethical matters.

Overall, Mufti Mahmood's works encompass a wide range of topics within Arabic literature, Islamic studies, and jurisprudence, showcasing his depth of knowledge and scholarly pursuits.

Mufti Mahmood's extensive literary output includes additional works in Arabic and Persian:

Arabic:
"Al Maqamat-al-Badriyya fi Milad-e Khairil Bariyya" - A work on the virtues of the Prophet Muhammad's birth, highlighting his reverence for the Prophet.

"Tanbeeh-al-Maftoon fil Firar-I-Anit Tawoon" - An admonition concerning fleeing from contagious diseases, reflecting his concern for public health and safety.

"Risalatun fi Iim-al-Hatati" - A treatise on the science of physiognomy, exploring the art of interpreting facial features.

"Risalatun fi Qaza-e-Sawm-e-Ramadhan" - A treatise on making up missed fasts in Ramadan, providing guidance on religious obligations.

"Hashiya ala Nukhbat-al-Fikr" - A commentary on "Nukhbat-al-Fikr," a seminal work in Islamic scholarship, demonstrating his dedication to elucidating complex texts for students' benefit.

"Fatwa fil Arbab-al-Mujaddidiya" - A fatwa regarding the Mujaddidiya spiritual order, showcasing his expertise in Islamic jurisprudence and Sufism.

"Al-Mutammima fi Sharh-al-Yateema" - A comprehensive commentary on Arabic syntax, indicating his proficiency in linguistic studies.

"Hashiya ala Shatibiyya" - A commentary on "Shatibiyya," a classical Arabic text, revealing his engagement with classical Islamic literature.

Persian:
"Risalah dar Halat-e-Amma" - A treatise on general conditions, likely addressing various social, cultural, or religious topics.

"Roznamcha-e-Haramain Shareefaln" - A diary or chronicle of his pilgrimage to the holy sites of Mecca and Medina.

"Roznamcha-e-Sarhind" - An account of his journey to Sarhind, possibly documenting his experiences and observations during his visit.

These works reflect Mufti Mahmood's erudition, encompassing diverse subjects within Islamic scholarship, spirituality, and practical guidance.

"Tarjuma-e-Bidayat al-Hidaya" - A translation of "Bidayat al-Hidaya," an influential work on Islamic jurisprudence and ethics, showcasing his commitment to making important texts accessible to Urdu-speaking audiences.

"Risalah dar Halat-e Ulama-e-Madras" - A treatise on the conditions and circumstances of the scholars in Madras, likely providing insights into the lives and challenges faced by scholars in the region.

"Risalah dar Fawaid-e-Mukhtalifa" - A treatise on various benefits or insights, possibly covering a range of topics related to Islamic scholarship, spirituality, or practical guidance.

In addition to his Arabic and Persian works, Mufti Mahmood authored several significant works in Urdu, including "Fathul Haq," "Saiful

Haq," "Nurul Fawaid," "Tuhfat-al-Hujjaj," "Riyazul Qurra," "Riyazul Momineen," "Khadim-al-Sunnah," and "Tabsirat-ur-Rashid." These works encompass diverse subjects such as Islamic theology, traditions, jurisprudence, and practical guidance.

Mufti Mahmood's dedication to completing his father and elder brother's commentary on the Quran is evident, although he too could not finish it. However, he left behind the monumental "Fatawa Mahmoodia," consisting of three large volumes containing his judicial decrees, demonstrating his expertise in Islamic law and jurisprudence.

Qazi Ubaidullah's contributions as a scholar and Qazi of Madras are notable, and his appointment to this prestigious position reflects his scholarly achievements. His memory and dedication to teaching in Madrasa-e-Muhammadi are commendable, and his recognition by the Indian Government with the title "Shamsul Ulama" underscores his scholarly prowess and contributions to society.

It seems you're providing information about Moulvi Abu Ahmad Muhammed Khaleelullah and his significant contributions as a scholar. Here's a summary of the information provided:

Moulvi Abu Ahmad Muhammed Khaleelullah, the youngest son of Qazi Badruddowlah, displayed remarkable scholarly achievements despite his young age when his father passed away. He was born on

25th Rabiul Awwal 1274 A.H. He migrated to Hyderabad and served there, leaving behind a legacy of authored works in Arabic, Persian, and Urdu. Some of his notable works include:

Al-Rowzat-al-Mukallala fil Ahadithal Musalsala

Takmilah-e-Jamut Jawame

Al-Salawat-al-Quraniya

Al-Salawat al Tayyabat ala Khair-il-Bariyyat

Hashiya Sharh-e-Tahzib

Hashiya-e-Rasheedia

He also authored works in Persian such as "Risalah-e-Lughat-e-Alf Laila," "Sharh Diwan-e-Mazhar," and "Nasayeh Namah." Additionally, he contributed to Urdu literature with works like "Kitab-al-Muta'llem," "Rabiul Anwar," "Gulzar-e-Saadat," "Chehal Hadith," and "Tuhfat-al-Zaireen."

Furthermore, Moulvi Abu Ahmad Muhammed Khaleelullah edited his judicial decrees, compiling them into a substantial volume of 552 pages.

Despite his early loss and young age, Moulvi Abu Ahmad Muhammed Khaleelullah's scholarly legacy endured, with his son, Dr. Muhammad Hameedullah, continuing his scholarly lineage.

Moulvi Qudrat Haleem and Moulvi Haji Abdur Rahman Saheb were both dedicated scholars who made significant contributions to literature and education. Here's a summary of their achievements:

Moulvi Qudrat Haleem:

Compiled several books in Persian and Urdu, including "Adab-al-Mureedeen," "Munajat-al-Qadri," "Riyazush Shuhada," "Islah-e-Ruhani," and "Tahseel-al-Manfaa bi Manaqib-al-Aimmat al-Arbaa." Printed and published works at Mazharul Ajaib Press and Muhammadi Press in Madras.

His scholarly endeavors enriched the literary landscape and promoted spiritual development.

Moulvi Haji Abdur Rahman Saheb:

Born on 12th Jamadı I 1282 A.H., he studied Arabic and Persian under renowned scholars such as Moulana Haji Mufti Mahmood, Shamsul Ulama Qazi Ubaidullah, and Moulvi Haji Muhammad Khaleelullah Saheb.

Achieved proficiency in calligraphy and restored numerous Arabic and Persian manuscripts, preserving them in his personal library.

Served as the Director and Teacher of Madrasa-e-Muhammadı from its establishment in 1309 A.H. until his demise on 29th Rajab 1352 A.H.

His dedication to education and preservation of manuscripts left a lasting impact on the intellectual heritage of the region.

Moulvi Ghulam Qadir was a renowned teacher of Arabic and Persian in Madras, known for his dedication to imparting Islamic sciences to students. His notable contributions include:

Miftah al-Salawt (مفتاح الصلوة):
Authored as a standard work on prayers in Persian, completed in 1261 A.H.Printed at Mazharul Ajaib Press, Madras, in 1278 A.H. Prescribed as a text for Islamic theology in Arabic Madrasas for an extended period.

Aqaid-e-Qadriya (عقايد قادريه):

A Persian translation of the Arabic work "Umdatul Kalam" (عمدة الكلام) by Abul Barakat Abdullah bin Ahmad bin Mahmood Nasafi. Divided into twenty-three sections (فصول), it comprehensively covers the Muslim creed and its various aspects.

Moulvi Ghulam Qadir's legacy lives on through his scholarly works, which continue to enrich the understanding of Islamic theology and practices.

His sons, Qazi Syed Maruf Albeez, Syed Ali Raza Albeez, and Syed Ghulam Rasool Albeez, continued his legacy of service in the field of Islamic knowledge and learning.

Moulvi Imamuddin Sharif Safi, a contemporary scholar, translated two preliminary texts, "Siratul Islam" and "Sirate Najat," from Persian into Urdu in 1286 A.H. These texts were originally derived from the Arabic work "Khulasatul Kaidani." Moulvi Sultan Mahmood, known by his pen name "Hamd," was a notable figure in Madras, composing poems in both Persian and Urdu. He passed away on March 1st, 1885.

Moulvi Qadir Basha Saheb, another prominent figure in Madras, was laid to rest on December 22nd, 1895, having made significant contributions to the city's intellectual landscape. Additionally, Qazi Syed Abdullah Khan Albeez, along with his sons, played vital roles in promoting Islamic knowledge and learning, with Qazi Syed Abdullah serving as the Qazi of Arcot for an extended period until his passing in 1285 A.H.

Syed Sadiq Hussaini Shareef, a renowned Persian and Urdu poet and educator, published several notable works including "Hadees-e-Shareef" in 1884, "Gulzar-e-Shareef" in 1875, "Sharaf-e-Urdu" in 1878, "Mathnawi-e-Sham-e-Ghurbat" in 1889, and his "Diwan" in 1887 and 1889. He preferred an independent life over employment, as expressed in his verse. He was the son of Ghulam Mohyuddin Naheef, known for his significant contributions to Persian grammar and commentary.

Moulvi Ghulam Dastageer Himmat was renowned as a Persian teacher, earning the title of "Shahr Ustad" (the city teacher) of Madras in 1291 A.H. He was highly respected, and students from various backgrounds sought to learn from him. His influence extended beyond teaching, as individuals aspiring to publish compositions often sought his approval.

He passed away on Wednesday the 10th Rajab 1322 A.H. 21st September 1904 A.D., commemorated in verse by Syed Shah Abdul Ghaffar Miskeen.

His sons, Muhammad Jafar Husaini Hareef and Ghulam Muhyuddin Saheb Haneef, were also esteemed poets in Persian and Urdu. Hareef's "diwan" was published in 1885 A.D., and he passed away a year later on Thursday the 2nd Jamadiul Awwal 1323 A.H. 6th July 1905 A.D.

Moulvi Hafiz Lutfullah Shams Quraishi served as a teacher for Urdu, alongside Moulvi Ghulam Dastageer Himmat's role as a Persian teacher in Madras. He died on Monday, the 10th Rajab 1333 A.H. 26th June 1915 A.D. His son, Moulvi Abdul Kareem succeeded him as the principal of the Madrasa-i-Islamia.

His contributions to Arabic, Persian, and Urdu education in South India were monumental, and his efforts in promoting Islamic studies among English students paved the way for greater cultural understanding and appreciation. Dr. Abdul Haq's legacy continues to inspire generations of scholars and educators in the field of Islamic studies and beyond management of its affairs. The Madrasa continued to function successfully, producing scholars and educators who made significant contributions to the fields of Arabic language and Islamic studies.

Students were encouraged to engage in public speaking and discussions through their own organizations, promoting their overall development. Affiliated with the University of Madras for Arabic and Persian examinations, students consistently excelled in Afzalul Ulama and Munshi Fazil examinations. Notable scholars such as Moulana Muhammad Shafee, Moulana Abdul Wahab, and Moulana Muhammad Usman Khan served as teachers, contributing to the academic excellence of the institution.

After the passing of Moulana Muhammad Fazlullah Saheb in 1912, Moulana Muhammad Ghazanfar Husain Shakir assumed the role of Principal, followed by Maulana Hafiz Abdul Wajid in 1951. Despite changes in leadership, the institution continues to thrive under Maulana Hafiz Abdul Wajid's guidance, maintaining its commitment to providing quality education.

Madrasa-i-Manbaul Anwar, Lalpet, established in 1864, stands out as an Arabic institution in South Arcot District. Reorganized in 1949, the medium of instruction is Tamil, catering to students primarily from Tamil Nadu. Under the leadership of Moulana Ziyauddin Amani, an accomplished poet in Arabic, Persian, and Urdu, the institution flourishes. His literary contributions include elegies, poems on the life of Prophet Muhammad, and critical works such as "Zajrul Umam an

Tarjumat-al-Quran bi Lisan-al-Ajam" in Urdu, addressing contemporary issues surrounding Quranic translation.

Jamia Mohammadia, Raidurug, established in 1926 by Moulana Syed Ismail Saheb, serves as a significant Arabic institution in Bellary District. Initially affiliated with Madras University and now with Sri Venkateswara University, Tirupati, it plays a crucial role in promoting Arabic and Persian education in Andhra Pradesh.

Additionally, three Oriental Arabic colleges in Kerala—Rawzat-ul-Uloom, Sullam-al-Salam, and Madeenatul Uloom—established in 1942, 1944, and 1946 respectively, contribute to the educational landscape of the state. These institutions play a vital role in nurturing Arabic scholarship and fostering academic excellence in Kerala.

The Oriental Arabic colleges in Kerala, previously affiliated with the University of Madras, are now affiliated with Kerala University, Trivandrum. These institutions attract a significant number of students, particularly from Malabar, who excel in Arabic studies. While Arabic remains a preferred choice, Persian language does not feature prominently in the curriculum of Kerala's Arabic Madrasas.

During the British era, the promotion of Arabic and Persian languages was evident in institutions like **Madrasa-e-Azam** and **Government Mohammadan College** (now Arts College) in Madras Presidency.

Notable figures like Moulvi Abdur Rahman Mabrur, a scholar and poet proficient in Persian and Urdu, contributed significantly to literary and academic circles. Upon the establishment of Government Mohammadan College in 1918, provisions were made for the study of Arabic, Persian, and Urdu languages. Professor Naeemurrahman of Allahabad played a crucial role in this regard. Dr. M. Abdul Haq, mentioned earlier, continued the effort to popularize these languages across South India. Other esteemed educators like Abdul Qadir, Hakeem Qadir, Moulana Syed Abdul Wahab Saheb Bukhari, Moulvi Raheem Ahmad Farooqi, S. M. Fazlullah Saheb, and S.A.Q. Hussaini contributed to the teaching of Arabic, Persian, Urdu, and Islamic History. Abdul Qadir, for instance, studied Arabic in Cairo and later served as a lecturer, preparing popular Arabic texts in Madras and Kerala.

Hakeem Qadir Ahmad was born in Madras in the late nineteenth century, where his grandfather, Hafiz Taqi Hussain, initiated his education. His father, Moulvi Muhyuddin Basha, a scholar of Arabic and Persian, guided him in his early studies. Hakeem Qadir Ahmad's educational journey began at Madrasa-e-Sayeedia, where he learned Persian from Syed Sadiq-al-Hussaini Shareef. Following the untimely death of his father, he continued his education at Madrasa-e-Nizamia in Hyderabad, studying Arabic, Persian, and Unani Medicine under renowned teachers. He furthered his medical education in Delhi and Lucknow before returning to Madras in 1918. There, he passed the

Afzalul Ulama examination and established a Unani dispensary named Qawmi Dawakhana. In 1922, he began teaching Arabic and Persian at Government Mohammadan College, serving for 25 years until his retirement. Despite retiring from teaching, he continued to practice as Unani physician until his passing in 1959. Hakeem Qadir Ahmad also contributed to scholarly works, editing and publishing Jami-ul-Ashya and Tibbe Fareedi with notes and introductions through the Government Oriental Manuscripts Library in Madras.

Moulana Syed Abdul Wahab Saheb Bukhari was born in Hyderabad in April 1902, into a family esteemed for its religious leadership, with his paternal grandfather serving as the preceptor of Nawab Mahboob Ali Khan of Hyderabad.

He pursued his education in Arabic and Persian at Madrasa Nizamia in Hyderabad for several years before joining Nizam College, where he studied English and other subjects for four years, eventually obtaining his M.A. Degree from Madras University in 1927. Subsequently, he earned the diploma of Afzalul Ulama in 1928 and completed his L.T. training in 1929.

Beginning his career as an Assistant Lecturer at Government Mohammadan College (now Arts College) in Madras from 1927 to 1930, he later assumed the Principal-ship of Madrasa-e-Jamalia, where he dedicated nine years to advancing Arabic education. Concurrently, he entered politics and served as a member of the Legislative Council of Madras for seven years, advocating for the application of Islamic Law of Inheritance to Muslim Mapillahs of Malabar.

Transitioning to educational leadership roles, Moulana Bukhari served as Principal of Islamia College, Vaniyambadi, from 1942 to 1944, followed by fourteen years as a Professor of Islamic History. Later, he became the principal of New College, Madras, serving on the Syndicate of Madras University for two terms before retiring in 1967 after a decade of service. He then assumed the position of U.G.C. Professor Principal of Jamalia Arabic College for five years.

In 1971, he submitted a thesis to U.G.C., New Delhi, on the "Contribution of India Muslim Law and Jurisprudence." Presently, he serves as the Honorary Director of Dairat-al Maarif Oosmania, Hyderabad.

Moulana Bukhari is renowned for his tireless efforts in awakening Muslims, having extensively traveled throughout South India and being actively involved in various associations and institutions. His eloquent speeches in English and Urdu, coupled with his amiable demeanor, have earned him the admiration of both Muslims and non-Muslims alike studies. He was known for his extensive knowledge and dedication to promoting Arabic, Persian, and Urdu languages without discrimination based on caste, creed, or community. His philanthropic endeavors extended to assisting the poor and needy from all walks of life.

With a deep commitment to Islamic scholarship, he made seven pilgrimages to Mecca and Medina, engaging in fruitful discussions with Arab leaders and scholars. His eloquence in Arabic garnered admiration, as demonstrated during his speech at the Al-Kindi celebrations in Baghdad in December 1962, where even General Qasim, the President of Iraq at the time, expressed astonishment at his command of the language.

Undertaking a "Goodwill Mission" to the Middle East in April-May 1964, he delivered speeches in Arabic and Persian at various venues, fostering goodwill and cultural exchange. Additionally, he authored an insightful book on the general history of Islam in English in 1942 and edited a Persian manuscript, "Baharistan-e-Sukhan," with accompanying notes and introduction, recently published by the Government Oriental Manuscripts Library, Madras.

His contributions to Islamic scholarship were further exemplified through a series of lectures delivered in English on Quran, Traditions, Islamic Law, Scholasticism, Mysticism, and modern challenges to Islam in September 1963, which were subsequently published.

Raheem Ahmad Farooqi, son of Moulana Qudrat Haleem Farooqi, pursued a similar path of scholarship, mastering Arabic, Persian, and English languages. He obtained degrees and diplomas from reputable institutions and served as a lecturer at Government Mohammadan College, Madras, contributing significantly to the advancement of Arabic, Persian, and Islamic studies.

Syed Muhammad Fazlullah, a distinguished scholar and poet, dedicated his life to the study and promotion of Arabic, Persian, and Urdu languages and literature. With a deep understanding of Arabic philology, he delved into extensive research on various subjects, including comparative linguistics between Arabic and English, Sufism, Islamic history, and numismatics related to the Umayyad and Abbasid periods.

His scholarly contributions extended to editing and publishing works such as "Safeenatun Najat" by Nawab Ghulam Ghouse Khan, focusing on maritime affairs. As a poet, he expressed his creativity in Persian and Urdu under the pen name Azad, showcasing his versatility and literary prowess.

Born in Madras in 1905, Syed Muhammad Fazlullah pursued his education in Persian and Urdu under renowned scholars like Prof. Naeemurrahman and Dr. M. Abdul Haq. He obtained his M.A. and L.T.

Degrees from the University of Madras, further enhancing his linguistic skills by studying French and German.

His career as a lecturer for Persian and Urdu at Government Arts College, as well as serving twice as its principal, reflects his commitment to education. He also served as the principal of Government Arts College, Ooty, before retiring in 1961. His dedication to academia continued as he served as a lecturer for Arabic at University College, Tirupati.

In his role as the Curator of the Government Oriental Manuscripts Library, Syed Muhammad Fazlullah spearheaded initiatives to publish valuable manuscripts in South Indian languages, including Arabic and Persian. His editorial work on Persian manuscripts, such as "Nuskha-e-Shahjahani" on cookery, contributed significantly to preserving and disseminating cultural heritage.

Syed Muhammad Fazlullah's legacy as a scholar and educator endures, leaving a lasting impact on the realms of language, literature, and cultural preservation. He passed away in Madras on 7th October 1966, leaving behind a rich intellectual heritage.

Muhammad Hafeezullah Khan Bahadur Hafiz Yar Jung authored "Tarikh-e-Hafeezullah Khani," a historical work of significance.

Additionally, he published "Diwan-e-Qurbi" with a valuable introduction.

Currently, he is dedicated to publishing "Muzakkir-e-Ahbab," which contains the life sketches of Persian poets from Samarqand and Bukhara, who thrived during the later half of the 9th century and the first half of the 10th century of the Islamic era.

Syed Abdul Qadir Husaini, hailing from a scholarly family in Qazi Mahalla, Medura, pursued his education in Arabic and Persian under various teachers. He earned his M.A. Degree in 1931 from the Madras University and served as a lecturer for Arabic and Islamic History at Government Arts College for an extended period. Known for his aptitude for research, he currently serves as the Lecturer for Islamic History at the University of Calcutta.

Throughout his career, Husaini has published numerous books in English after thorough studies of Arabic and Persian historical sources. Some of his notable works include:

"Ibn Arabi" (1931): A concise yet comprehensive work on the life and works of the renowned mystic Shaikh Muhyuddin Ibn Arabi, published by Theosophical Society, Adayar.

"Arab Administration" (1949)

"Administration under the Mughals" (1952)

"Constitution of the Arab Empire" (1950, published in 1954)

"Arab History"

"Bahman Shah" (1960), for which he obtained a Ph.D. degree from Dacca.

Syed Abdul Qadir Husaini passed away in Calcutta on 10th April 1966, leaving behind a significant legacy in the field of Islamic history and scholarship completed his M.A. in Arabic and Persian. He served as a Lecturer at various institutions, including Government Arts College, Madras, and Government Brennen College, Tellicherry. Additionally, he worked as an Assistant Librarian at the Government Oriental Manuscripts Library, where he contributed to the descriptive catalogue of Arabic and Persian manuscripts.

A skilled orator, Moulana P. Habeeb Khan Saheb was well-versed in the science of Tradition and often incorporated them into his speeches delivered in Arabic, Persian, and Urdu. He also edited "Sawanihat-e-Mumtaz" by Khursheedul Mulk Bahadur, which was published from the Government Oriental Manuscripts Library, Madras.

Tragically, while preparing to deliver a speech on the life and works of an esteemed figure on the night of Friday, 17th July 1964, Moulana P. Habeeb Khan Saheb suffered a heart attack and passed away before medical assistance could be provided. He was laid to rest in Rama Rau Bagh on the evening of 18th July 1964, leaving behind a legacy of scholarship and dedication to Arabic and Persian studies. In Arabic and

Persian, he joined the Oriental Research Institute as a Senior Lecturer. His colleague, Muhammad Munawwar Khan Gawhar, also contributed significantly to the advancement of Arabic, Persian, and Urdu studies at the Institute.

The establishment of the Oriental Research Institute marked a significant milestone in the promotion and preservation of classical languages, including Arabic and Persian, along with regional languages like Tamil, Telugu, Malayalam, and Kannada. The institute aimed to uncover and highlight notable literary works in these languages, thereby enriching cultural and academic discourse.

Syed Muhammad Husain Nainar's background in Arabic and Persian studies, coupled with his tenure at the Government Arts College, Madras, equipped him with the expertise to contribute meaningfully to the research and academic activities of the Oriental Research Institute. Similarly, Muhammad Munawwar Khan Gawhar's appointment as a Junior Lecturer further strengthened the institute's efforts in promoting linguistic and literary studies in Arabic, Persian, and Urdu.

Overall, the Oriental Research Institute played a crucial role in fostering scholarship and preserving the rich cultural heritage embodied in classical languages, including Arabic and Persian, within the academic landscape of the University of Madras and beyond renowned personalities of South India, particularly of Madras city. He was born at Madras on the 8th Rabiul Awwal, 1303 A.H. and died on the 23rd Rajab, 1383 A.H. (21st August 1963).

Muhammad Munawwar Khan Gawhar received his early education at home and then joined the Government Arts College, Madras, for his higher studies. He excelled in Arabic, Persian, and Urdu languages and literature. Later, he pursued higher education at Aligarh Muslim University, where he obtained his M.A. LL.B. degrees.

His academic pursuits led him to London, where he conducted research on "Arab Geographers' Knowledge of South India" and earned his Ph.D. from Oxford University. Proficient in multiple languages including Arabic, Persian, Urdu, Tamil, Malayalam, French, German, and English, Gawhar's linguistic versatility facilitated his scholarly endeavors.

During his tenure as a Senior Lecturer, Reader, and Professor at the University of Madras, Gawhar made significant contributions to academic scholarship. He authored the five-volume series "Sources of the Nawabs of Carnatic," shedding light on South Indian history. Additionally, he translated "Tuhfat-al-Mujahideen" into English and published the original text in the Annals of Oriental Research, University of Madras.

Gawhar's contributions extended to Tamil literature, where he published works such as "Sydakkadi Vallal" and "Nondi Natakam," earning recognition as a Tamil scholar and writer. His efforts also included editing the Tamil classic poem "Sira Puranam" with a comprehensive commentary in Tamil.

Passionate about bringing recognition to eminent South Indian scholars in Arabic and Persian, Gawhar supervised the editing and publication of the works of Mir Ismail Khan Abjadi, further enriching scholarly discourse.

Despite his retirement, Gawhar remained committed to academic pursuits, serving as the Assistant Director of All India Radio's Indonesian Unit in New Delhi. His vision for establishing an Arabic Madrasa in his native place remained unfulfilled due to his untimely demise on September 23, 1963. He was laid to rest at the Walajahi Mosque campus in Madras, leaving behind a legacy of scholarly contributions and a profound impact on South Indian academia.

Najaf Ali Khan, a distinguished poet in Persian, authored two mathnawis, "Baharia" and "Khizania," portraying the beauty of the Spring and Autumn seasons. Additionally, he provided annotations for the "Mathnawi" of "Sikander Nama." Athima, his wife, was also a talented poetess who composed four mathnawis: "Gulshan-e-

Shahidan," "Culshan-e-Mahrukhan," "Jahan-e-Fireb," and "Nasab Nama."

Abdul Ghani, Gawhar's father, contributed to Persian literature with works like "Anwar-i-Azeem" and "Nazm-e-Dilchasp-e-Aruir." Abdus Samad Khan Mahir, Gawhar's uncle, composed lyrical poems and qaseedas in Persian, publishing them under the titles "Qasaid-e-Mahir" and "Diwan-e-Farsi."

Gawhar himself was born in 1873 and studied Arabic and Persian under his father and other teachers. He published his compositions in Persian as "Makhzan-e-Saadat" and contributed extensively to research about Persian and Urdu poets of the Deccan, which were published by the University of Madras under the title "Sukhanwaran-e-Buland Fikr" in 1936.

Gawhar passed away in 1942 in Hyderabad. His younger brother, Shamsul Ulama Moulvi Muhammad Abdur Rahman Saheb Shatir, also made significant contributions to Urdu literature by publishing mathnawis of high quality.

Moulana Muhammad Husain Mahvi Siddiqul, born in Lucknow in 1888, served as a Junior Lecturer for Urdu at the Department of Arabic, Persian, and Urdu in the Oriental Research Institute. He retired in April 1949 after contributing significantly to the field. His works, including editing and publishing various books, such as "Anwarnamah" by Mir Asmail Khan Abjadi and "Mathnawi Mawaddat Nama" by Mir Ismail Khan Abjadi, were published by the University after his retirement. He also edited and published Urdu works like "Diwan-i-Azfari," "Diwan-e-Bedar," and "Waqiat-e-Azfari."

Moulana Mahvi is currently residing in Bhopal, continuing his literary pursuits and contributions to Urdu literature.

Abu Hashim Syed Usha, born in Hyderabad on August 1, 1903, obtained his B.A. degree from the Muslim University, Aligarh, in 1927. Before joining the Department of Arabic, Persian, and Urdu at the University of Madras, he authored a critical work on the renowned Persian poet Hafiz Shirazi. During his tenure, he made significant contributions, retiring as Reader and Head of the Department on July 31, 1963. Among his notable works edited under the auspices of the University of Madras are:

"Futuh-al-Salatin" by Isami, offering an authentic history of India in Persian verse from Sultan Mahmood of Ghazni to Muhammad bin Tughlaq, published in 1948.

"Diwan-e-Awhadi" by Awhadi of Maragha, published in 1951.

"Diwan-e-Ubayd Zakani," published in 1952.

"Fathnama-e-Mahmood Shahi," a historical treatise in Persian verse detailing an expedition led by Mahmood Shah Bahmani II, composed by Ayant of Bidar, published in 1955.

"Kanz-al-Fawaid," a valuable work on poetics, rhetoric, and prosody in Persian by Husain Muhammad Shah Shihab Ansari, published in an unknown year.

"Taimur Nama," a history of Taimur in Persian verse by Abdullah Hatifi, published in 1958.

Additionally, he edited:
"Tarikh-e-Shahjahan" by Farid Bhakkarl.

"Padshah Nama" by Iradat Khan.

Abu Hashim Syed Usha's editorial endeavors also include:

"Selections of Jawamiul Hikayat" by Awfi.

"Waqa-e-Muhammad Shah Badshah" by Nadir Shah.

"Shigarf Nama" by Itusanuddin.

"Tarikh-e-Khan-e-Jahani" by Abbas Sarwani and others, which are awaiting publication.

Furthermore, he is currently involved in the writing of a commentary on the Quran.

It's evident from the general survey that Arcot, Vellore, Madras, and Natharnagar have been significant centers of Arabic and Persian learning for the past two hundred and fifty years. The natural aptitude and liking for these languages among Muslims have persisted, and now, with the strengthening of political and cultural ties between India and the Middle East after independence, even non-Muslims are showing great interest in learning Arabic and Persian. Arabic, in particular, is gaining popularity, with the introduction of an M.A. course in Arabic at New College, Madras since 1955, and increasing admissions at the P.U.C. and B.A. levels. This trend suggests a bright future for Arabic in South India.

Conclusion:

In conclusion, the passages presented here offer a fascinating glimpse into the enduring legacy of Arabic and Persian scholarship in South India. From the humble beginnings in historic towns to the modern resurgence in educational institutions, these languages have continued to captivate the hearts and minds of learners across generations. As we reflect on the rich tapestry of cultural exchange and intellectual pursuit, it becomes evident that Arabic and Persian hold a cherished place in the mosaic of India's diverse heritage. Looking ahead, it is heartening to witness the growing interest and enthusiasm for these languages, signaling a promising future for Arabic and Persian studies in South India. As custodians of this rich legacy, may we continue to nurture and celebrate the beauty and wisdom encapsulated within the realms of Arabic and Persian language and literature.

Bibliography

Al-Attas, S. M. N. (1993). Islam and secularism. Kuala Lumpur: ISTAC.

Al-Dimasyqi, A.-I. A.-N. (2016). Syarh Shahih Muslim. Dar al-Kutub al-`Ilmiyah.

Allen, C. (2013). Islamophobia. In Islamophobia. https://doi.org/10.4324/9781315745077-41

al-Maraghi, M. (2002). Tafsir al-Maraghi. Beirut: Darul Fikir.

Al-Qaradawi, Y. (2010). Islam an introduction. Kuala Lumpur: Islamic Book Trust.

al-Qurtubi, A. A. M. ibn A. (2014). Tafsir al-Qurtubi (Vol. 20). Beirut: Dar al-Kutub al-'Ilmiyah.

Al-Qushayri, I. (2018). Tafsir al-Qushayri. Dar Ihya' al-Turath al-Arabi.

Al-Rāzī, F. (2000). Al-Tafsīr al-Kabīr aw Mafātih al-Gayb, Vol. VII. Dar Al-Hadith.

Al-Sya'rawi, A.-I. A.-M. (2007). Tafsir Al-Sya'rawi. Qitha' al-Saqafah wa al-Kutub.

Al-Syawkani, M. bin A. (2014). Fath al-Qadir al-Jami' baina Fannai al-Riwayah wa al-Dirayah min 'Ilm al-Tafsir, Vol. 5. Dar Ibnu Hazim.

Al-Thabathaba'i. (1987). Tafsir Al-Mizan. Islamic Publications Office.

Al-Zuhaily, W. (2009). Al-Tafsir al-Munir fi al-Aqidah wa al-Syariah wa al-Manhaj. Dar al-Fikr.

APS (Applied Social Psychology). (2017). The Role of Religion in Prejudice Enablement and Reduction. Retrieved December 26, 2022, from https://sites.psu.edu/aspsy/2017/09/28/the-role-of-religion-in-prejudice-enablement-and-reduction/

Bakhshi Hazrat 'Alī Aḥmed and Rizwānur Raḥmān. (2012). Glimpses of the Holy Qur'ān. (New Delhi: Adam Publishers and Distributors).

Chelini-Pont, B. (2013). Relationship between Stereotyping and the Place of Religion in the Public Sphere. In J. Svartvik, Jesper & Wiren (Ed.), Religious Stereotyping and Interreligious Relations (pp. 75–84). Palgrave Macmillan.

Geertz, C. (1977). The Interpretation of Cultures. Basic Books.

Geertz, C. (2013). Religion as a cultural system. In Anthropological Approaches to the Study of Religion (pp. 1–46). https://doi.org/10.4324/9781315017570

Hanafi, H. (2000). Islam in the modern world: Religion, ideology and development vol. I. Cairo: Dar Kabaa.

Hanafi, H. (2006). Culture and civilizations, conflict or dialogue? Vol. I the meridian thought. Cairo: Book Center for Publishing.

Jafari, F. (2020). Theological knowledge in Islamic mysticism and gnosticism." Kanz Philosophia A Journal for Islamic Philosophy and Mysticism 6(2). DOI: https://doi.org/10.20871/kpjipm.v6i2.92.

Karama, M. J., & Khater, N. A. (2020). Educational peace theory in the holy qur'an. Al-Bayān – Journal of Qur'ān and Ḥadīth Studies, 18, 138–154.
http://scholar.ppu.edu/bitstream/handle/123456789/2214/1.pdf?sequence=1&isAllowed=y

Khairulnizam, M., & Saili, S. (2009). Inter-faith dialogue: The qur'anic and prophetic perspective. Journal of Usuluddin, 9(2), 65–94.

Khaldun, I. (2015). Muqaddimah. Cairo: Dar-Ibnu al-Aitam.

Kidwai, Salim. (1996). Hindustani Mufassirein Awr Unki' Arabi Tafsirein (in Urdu) .(New Delhi:Maktaba Jamiah).

Kokan, Moḥammad Yousuf. (1960). Arabic and Persian in Carnatic, (Madras: Hafiza House).

Ma'roof M M M. (1995). *Spoken Tamil dialect of the Muslims of Sri Lanka: Language as Identity classifier*. Islamic Studies 34 (4).

Nashir, H. (2015). Understanding the ideology of Muhammadiyah. Muhammadiyah University Press.

Nieuwkerk, K. van, LeVine, M., & Stokes, M. (2016). Islam and popular culture. University of Texas Press.

Patji, A. R. (1991). The Arabs of Surabaya: a study of sociocultural integration. Canberra: Australian National University.

Putra, A. D., Purnomo, D., & Utomo, A. W. (2019). Sociological study of harmony in diversity: Lessons from Salatiga. Walisongo: Jurnal Penelitian Sosial Keagamaan, 27(1), 69–98. 10.21580/ws.27.1.3504

Ridwan, M., & Robikah, S. (2019). Ethical vision of the qur'an: Interpreting concept of the qur'anic sociology in developing religious harmony. Jurnal Ilmiah Islam Futura, 18(2), 308–326. http://dx.doi.org/10.22373/jiif.v19i2.5444

Sanaa Sha'lan, 'Adore Me'(A'shaquni), Daira al- Maktaba al-Wataniyya, Hashemite Kingdom of Jordan, Third Edition, 2016.

Saerozi, M. (2017). Dynamics of the development of istiqomah mosque in front of a church in Ungaran Central Java Indonesia. Journal of Indonesian Islam, 11(02), 423–458. 10.15642/JIIS.2017.11.2.423-458

Saged, A. A. (2021). Honoring the human self with a world peace study in the light of purposes the holy quran. Quranika: Journal of Libahuts Qur'an, 19(2), 223–234.

Shareef, Moḥammed Muṣṭafa and Bad'iuddin Ṣabri. (2008). Development of Tafseer Literature in India, (Hyderabad: Osmania University).

Shihab, M. Q. (2004). Tafsir al-mishbah. Jakarta: Lentera Hati.

Shu'aib, Tayka. (1993). Arabic, Arwi and Persian in Sarandib and Tamil Nadu, (Chennai: Imaamul Aroos Trust).

Thabari, I. J. (1999). Tafsir al Thabari. Kairo: Dar al Fikr.

Zamakhsyari, M. I. U. al. (2012). Al-kassyaf 'an haqaiq al-tanzil wa 'uyun al-ta'wil fi wujuh al-ta'wil. Cairo: Dar al-Hadis.

Zubair, K M A Aḥamed. (2010). *Tamil-Arabic Relationship*, ed. John Samuel G, (Chennai:The Institute of Asian Studies Press).

Zubair, K M A Ahamed. (2012). *Eminent Scholars of Sheik Sadaqathullah Appa's Family and their contribution to Arabic and Islamic Studies,* (in Arabic), Thaqafatul ḥind 54, (3&4).

Zubair, K M A Ahamed. (2013). *Qasaid al-Madaih al-Nabaviyya fi Tamil Nadu,* (in Arabic), Thaqafatul ḥind 64, (4).

Zubair, K M A Aḥamed. (2017). Prophet's Panegyrics in Arabic Literature, (Moldova: Lambert Academic Publishing).

Printed by Books on Demand GmbH, Norderstedt / Germany